COPTIC ORTHODOX PATRIARCHATE

MANY YEARS

WITH PEOPLE'S QUESTIONS

PART ONE

Biblical Questions

By

H.H. POPE SHENOUDA III

Title	: So Many Years with the Problems of People. Part I - Biblical Questions.
Author	: H. H. Pope Shenouda III.
Translated By	: St. George Coptic Orthodox Church Chicago, Illinios.
Revised By	: Mrs. Wedad Abbas
Illustrated By	: Sister Sawsan.
Edition	: The second of February, 1993.
Typesetting	: J.C. Center, Heliopolis.
Printing	: Dar El Tebaa El Kawmia, Cairo.
Legal Deposit No.	: 3035/1993.
Revised	: COEPA - 1997

H.H. Pope Shenouda III
117th Pope and Patriarch of Alexandria
and the See of St Mark

CONTENTS

INTRODUCTION

1. Days of Creation and Geology (Gen. 1)
2. When was the Light Created? (Gen. 1)
3. Is Earth Part of the Sun? (Gen. 1)
4. About the Creation of Man (Gen. 1 & 2)
5. The Sons of God and the Sons of Men (Gen. 6:2)
6. Maker of Peace and Creator of Evil (Is. 45:7)
7. What is the Meaning of "Buy A Sword"? (Luke 22:36)
8. The Three Questions of Abraham (Gen. 18:2)
9. All who Ever Came Before Me are Thieves and Robbers (John 10:8)
10. The Iniquity of the Fathers on the Children (Ex. 20:5)
11. The Commendation of the Unjust Steward (Luke 16:8)
12. This Generation Passed Away (Matt. 24:34)
13. The Blasphemy Against the Holy Spirit (Matt. 12:31)
14. What is the Book of Jasher? (Josh. 10:13)

15. The Appearance of the Lord to Saul (Acts 9 & 22)
16. Christ Before the Thirtieth
17. Little of Wine (1 Tim. 5:23)
18. The Potter and the Clay (Rom. 9:20-21)
19. Is This Metempsychosis? (Matt. 11:14)
20. The Meaning of the "Mammon of Unrighteousness" (Luke 16:9)
21. Why Forgive Them? (Luke 23:34)
22. The Meaning of Salah, Maran-A'Tha, Anathema, Kedar
23. The Rich and the Entering of the Kingdom (Mark 10:24)
24. Which Heaven Did They Ascend To? (John 3:13)
25. Was the Sin of Adam, Adultery? (Gen. 3:2)
26. Who Is Melchizedek? (Gen. 14; Heb. 7)
27. Do Not Be Overly Righteous (Eccl. 7:16)
28. Did Judas Partake of the Holy Communion? (Mark 14; John 13)
29. Were Solomon and Samson Saved? (Heb. 11; 2 Sam. 7)
30. The Meaning of "Be Angry, and Do Not Sin (Ps. 4; Rom. 12)
31. Did One or Both Thieves Blaspheme? (Matt 27:44)
32. Did the Baptist Doubt? (Luke 7:19)
33. But A Sword (Matt. 10:34)

34. Was the Plucking of the Corn Ears, Stealing? (Mark 2:23)
35. For in Much Wisdom is Much Grief (Eccl. 1:18)
36. Are All Equal? (Matt. 20:1-14)
37. Is It Our Daily Bread or Our Bread For the Morrow? (Matt. 6:11)
38. Will Not Taste Death Till (Mark 9:1)
39. Signs of the End of the World (Matt. 24; 2 Thess.)
40. The Account of the Death of Moses the Prophet (Deut. 34:5)

INTRODUCTION

The history of questions with me is lengthy. Since I have been ordained a Bishop on September 30,1962, over twenty-five years ago, I adopted a specific method in teaching and preaching: to give a chance for the audience to introduce their questions and have them answered before the beginning of the main lecture.

This way thousands of questions accumulated before me during the thousands of lectures that I have given, in the weekly spiritual meetings, on Friday evenings; the Bible study meetings on Tuesday (1968-1972); the theological lectures on Wednesday; my meetings with the priests; with the Sunday school teachers and their conferences; the meetings of college societies; general meetings in Alexandria, on Sunday; the lectures that were given in the theological seminary in Alexandria and Cairo; or the spiritual meetings during my visits to churches and dioceses.

Even before my monastic life, I used to answer the spiritual questions of the readers of the Sunday school magazine and the questions followed me everywhere, even in the monastery.

The questions varied some around biblical verses, some about theology, doctrines, ministry, spiritual life or social relationships and many other subjects.. I excluded what was repetitious, personal, or what I answered with one sentence or a joke.

I chose what was fit from the questions for publication, so the people would not have to ask the same questions again and to have almost uniform answers to such questions.

Pope Shenouda III

[1]

DAYS OF CREATION AND GEOLOGY

Question

How can the saying of the Bible that God created the world in six days coincide with the opinion of the geologists that the age of the earth is thousands even millions of years?

Answer:

The days of creation are not Solar days as our days now.

The day of creation is a period of time, not known how long, which could haven been a second or thousands or millions of years. This period was determined by the saying "so the evening and the morning were..."

The evidences for this are many, among which are:

1. **The Solar day** is the period of time between the sunrise and its rising again or between the sunset and its setting again. **Since the sun was only created on the fourth day *(Gen. 1:16-19).*, then the first four days were not solar days**.

2. **As for the seventh day, the Bible did not state that it has ended.**

The Bible did not say [so the evening and the morning were the seventh day], and thousands of years passed from Adam till now while this seventh day is still going on. Accordingly, the days of creation are not Solar days but unknown periods of time.

3. As a whole, the Bible said about all the creation and its six days: *". This is the history of the heavens and the earth when they were created, in the day that the LORD God made the earth and the heavens," (Gen. 2:4).*

So the Bible summed up in the word (day) all the six days of creation...

Let the geologists say then whatever they want about the age of the earth; for the Bible did not mention any age for the earth that may contradict the views of the geologists.

The way the Lord looks to the measurement of time is explained by the apostle as follows: *"With the Lord one day is as a thousand years, and a thousand years as one day " (2 Pet. 3:8).*

[2]

WHEN WAS THE LIGHT CREATED?

Question

The Book of Genesis states that God created the light on the first day (Gen 1:3), while it states that the sun, moon and stars were created on the fourth day (Gen. 1:14-18). What is the difference between the two matters?

And was the light created on the first day or the fourth?

Answer:

God created light on the first day as the Bible indicated. But, what light? It is the substance of light, the shining mass of fire from which God made the sun, the moon and the stars on the fourth day. On the fourth day also God established the astronomical laws and the permanent relation between these celestial bodies...

[3]

IS THE EARTH PART OF THE SUN

Question:

I have read in a book a criticism of the story of creation as mentioned in the first chapter of the Book of Genesis. How can the earth be part of the sun as the scientists say, while the Bible states that the sun was created on the fourth day after the creation of the earth? So how can the earth be part of something that was created later on?!

Answer:

Scientists do not say that the earth was part of the sun and separated from it, otherwise the sun will be missing this portion.

What scientists say is that earth is part of the solar system and not of the sun itself. It was part of the Nebula; that fiery mass which was no doubt luminous. This Nebula is what the Bible meant by saying on the first day *"Then God said, let there be light, and there was light."*

Earth was part of this mass and separated from it. The earth gradually cooled down until its surface became completely cool and on the third day became fit to grow plants and trees on, using the light and heat radiating from the Nebula.

On the fourth day, from this mass God created, the sun, moon, stars, meteors and all other celestial bodies and regulated the interrelations and the movement of these bodies.

The sun, on the fourth day, remained as it is; a whole with the earth attached to it, but God set the relation between earth and sun, moon and other stars and planets through the astronomical laws.

[4]

ABOUT THE CREATION OF MAN

Question:

In Genesis there are two stories about the creation of man, the first is in the first chapter where God created man; male and female, and the second is in the second chapter where Adam and Eve were created. Do these two accounts coincide with each other.

Answer:

The story of making man is one story for the same man.

The account is mentioned as a whole in the first chapter but in detail in the second chapter.

In the first chapter, the making of man was part of all the process of creation. Then the details came in the second chapter about how Adam was created of dust then God breathed into his nostrils the breath of life; how Eve was created from one of Adams'ribs. It also mentioned the feelings of Adam before and after making Eve and giving Adam and Eve their names.

The two accounts are integral; in the first you find the given blessing and the allowed foods and in the second you find how they were created, the names given to them and a hint about Paradise.

[5]

THE SONS OF GOD AND THE SONS OF MEN

Question:

(Gen. 6:2) describes before the account of the flood *"that the sons of God saw the daughters of men, that they were beautiful,. and they took wives for themselves of all whom they chose."* Who are the sons of God? and who are the daughters of men?

Answer:

The sons of God are the descendants of Seth and the daughters of men are the descendants of Cain.

After the slaying of Abel the righteous, Adam begot another son and named him Seth, *"for God has appointed another seed for me instead of Abel"* (Gen. 4:25) *"And as for Seth, to him also a son was born; and he named him Enosh. Then men began to call on the name of the LORD."* (Gen. 4:26). In the genealogy of Jesus Christ it is mentioned that *"the son of Enosh, the son of Seth, the son of Adam, the son of God."* (Luke 3:38).

The sons of Seth were called the sons of God for they were the sanctified offspring from which Noah came, then Abraham, then David, then Christ through whom all the tribes of the earth were blessed. They are the believers that belong to God; those took the blessing of Adam *(Gen. 1:28)* and then the blessing of Noah *(Gen. 9:1)*.

It was good that God called some humans His sons before the flood.

The sons of Cain were not attributed to God for the curse that befell Cain, befell them also *(Gen. 4:11)* and they walked in the way of corruption so they were called the sons of men and they all drowned by the flood.

[6]

MAKER OF PEACE AND CREATOR OF EVIL

Question:

Isn't God the absolute goodness? How then is it said about Him that He is the maker of peace and creator of evil (Is. 45:7) while evil doesn't agree with God's nature.

Answer:

We should know first the meaning of the word "good" and the word "evil" in the biblical terminology for they have more than one meaning.

The word "evil" could mean sin which is not the case in the verse *"creator of evil"* in *(Is. 45:7).*

"Evil" meaning sin doesn't agree with the goodness of the Lord for He is the absolute goodness. But it comes also in the Bible to mean tribulations and hardships.

The word "good" has also two contradicting meanings: it could mean righteousness - opposite of sin, and it could mean opposite of tribulations - richness, blessing, abundance and various kinds gifts.

* This is very clear in the story of Job the Righteous, when the tribulations befell him and his wife grumbled, he rebuked her saying " *"You speak as one of the foolish women speaks. Shall we indeed accept good from God, and shall we not accept adversity?" (Job. 2:10).*

Job did not mean by the word "evil" here "sin"; for no sin befell him from the Lord but he meant by evil the tribulations he underwent.

As for the death of his children, the destruction of his house and the plundering of his oxen, donkeys, sheep and camels, all these tribulations and calamities commonly known as evil, the Bible says *" when Job's three friends heard of all this adversity that had come upon him, each one came from his own place; to mourn with him and to comfort him." (Job.2:11)*

With the same concept the Lord had spoken about His punishment for the people of Israel saying *"'Behold, I will bring calamity on this place and on its inhabitants, all the curses that are written in the book" (2 Chr. 34:24).* Surely the Lord here did not mean by evil the sin.

What He meant by evil was the captivity of the children of Israel, their defeat before their enemies and the other afflictions that He brought upon them to punish them.

* Another example is the saying of the Lord about Jerusalem *"Behold, I will bring such a catastrophe on this place, that whoever hears of it, his ears will tingle "* (Jer. 19:3) The Lord mentioned the details of that evil saying *"I will cause them to fall by the sword before their enemies... their corpses I will give as meat for the birds of the heavens and for the beasts of the earth. I will make this city desolate and a hissing... even so I will break this people and this city, as one breaks a potter's vessel, which can not be made whole again"* (Jer. 19:7-11).

* The same meaning is given in the Book of Amos. *(Amos 9:4).*

* In the promises of the Lord to rescue the people of Israel from captivity, difficulties and defeat "For thus says the LORD: *'Just as I have brought all this great calamity on this people, so I will bring on them all the good that I have promised them."* (Jer. 32:42) the word evil meant captivity and the promise was to return them from captivity.

The word "good" here does not mean righteousness or godliness as it is also clear that the word "evil" here did not mean sin.

The word good means also blessings, wealth, and prosperity.

The Psalm says *" Who satisfies your mouth with good things, So that your youth is renewed like the eagle's" (Ps. 103:5)* and the Lord says in *(Jer. 5:25) " Your iniquities have turned these things away, And your sins have withheld good from you."*

In the same meaning also it is said about the Lord that He is *"the maker of good and creator of evil"* which means He gives the blessings and prosperity and also He allows afflictions and adversities.

If the word evil means afflictions, then it can be from God. He wants or allows it as a discipline for people or to urge them to repent or for any spiritual benefit that might be gained from these afflictions *(James 1:2-4).*

The phrase "creator of evil" or "maker of evil" means whatever the people regard as evil or trouble or tribulation which also might be for good.

Examples for good in the sense of righteousness, and for evil in the sense of sin:

+ *" for the punishment of evildoers and for the praise of those who do good." (1 Pet. 2:14).*

+ Also *"Depart from evil, and do good. " (Ps. 34:14).*

+ And the saying of the Lord *" your little ones and your children, who you say will be victims, who today have no knowledge of good and evil" (Deut. 1:39)* and also the verse *"the tree of knowledge of good and evil" (Gen. 2:9).*

Accordingly the verse *"He treated him well"* means helped him, aided, rescued, had mercy and gave him good gifts and presents.

On the other hand the verse *"you meant evil against me"* means to harm him.

When the Lord brings evil on a nation, it means put them under the rod of correction by tribulations and plagues which are considered evil.

[7]

WHAT IS THE MEANING OF "BUY A SWORD"?

Question:

How can the Lord Christ he the maker of peace and the king of peace, and at the same time tell His disciples *"he who has no sword let him sell his garment and buy one." (Luke 22:36)*

"What did He mean by ordering His disciples to buy a sword? Why when they told Him *"here are two swords* **He replied** *"it is enough." (Luke 22:38).*

Answer:

The Lord Christ absolutely did not mean the sword in its literal sense.

As an evidence of that, hours after He said this statement, and during His arrest *"Simon Peter, having a sword, drew it and struck the high priest servant and cut off his ear... then Jesus said to Peter: put your sword into the sheath" (John 18:10-11)*, "for all who take the sword will perish by the sword. " (Matt. 26:51-52). If the Lord was asking them to use the sword, he would not have stopped Peter from using the sword in such circumstances.

But the Lord meant the symbolic meaning of the sword which is the spiritual struggle.

The Lord was talking to them on his way to Gethsemane (Luke 22:39) in His last minutes before His arrest to be crucified. He said *"Let him sell his garments and buy a sword"* then right after that He said *'for I say to you that this which is written must still be accomplished in Me", "and He was numbered with the transgressors"(Luke 22:37)*.
What is the common line between these two statements? It seems as if He was telling them, while I was with you, I guarded you, I was the sword that protected you, but now I am going to give myself up in the hands of sinners and the saying *"numbered with transgressors"* will be fulfilled... then take care of yourselves and struggle.

Since I am going to leave you, every one of you should fight the spiritual fight, and buy a sword.

St. Paul had spoken about "the sword of the spirit" in his epistle to the Ephesians and about: *"the whole armour of God, the breast plate of righteousness, and the shield of faith" (Eph. 6:11-17)*. That is what the Lord Christ meant by that; so we might be able to be steadfast in face of the snares of Satan in these spiritual fights.

The disciples did not understand that spiritual symbol at that time so they answered: here are two swords.

As He told them before in the same symbolic concept *"Beware of the leaven of the Pharisees" (Luke 21:1),* He meant their hypocrisy but they thought He spoke about the bread *(Mark 8:17).* In the same manner they answered Him, when He talked to them about the sword of the spirit, here are two swords, so He replied that "It is enough"... It is enough discussion in this subject since there wasn't enough time... He did not mean the swords by the statement "It is enough" otherwise He would say they are enough...

We should distinguish between what the Lord meant to be understood symbolically and what literally. The flow of the conversation usually indicates that.

[8]

THE THREE GUESTS OF ABRAHAM

Question:

Who were the three that Abraham the patriarch hosted in Genesis 18? Were they the Holy Trinity? Was Abraham's worshipping them an indication of that? He talked to them at times in plural and at other times in singular, is that a proof for the Trinity?

Answer:

We cannot say that these three were the Holy Trinity.

For there is no clear separation in the Trinity as it is the case here. The Son says *"I and My Father are One."* *(John 10:30)* and says *"I am in the Father, and the Father in Me; He who has seen Me has seen the Father"* *(John 14:9-10)* and it was also said about the Father *"no one has ever seen God"* *(John 1:18)*.

The prostration of Abraham was the prostration of respect, not of worshipping. As Abraham bowed himself before the sons of Heth when he bought from them the Cave of Machpelah *(Gen. 23:7)*.

If Abraham had known that he was before the Lord, he would not have offered them butter, milk, bread and meat and said *"rest yourselves under the tree. And I will bring a morsel of bread that you may refresh your hearts. After that you may pass by. " (Gen. 18:4-8).*

The three were the Lord and with Him two angels.

The two angels, after the meeting, went on to Sodom *(Gen. 18:16 & 22; Gen. 19:1)* and Abraham remained standing before the Lord *(Gen. 18:22)* interceding for Sodom *(Gen. 18:23)*.

When our father Abraham saw these three men, while he was sitting at the tent door, they surely were not in the same magnificence or reverence. The Lord no doubt was distinguished from the angels in reverence and glory, and perhaps the two angels were walking behind Him.

Therefore our father Abraham talked to the Lord in the singular considering Him the representative of this group.

He said to Him *"My Lord, if I have now found favour in Your sight, do not pass on by Your servant. Please let a little water be brought, and wash your feet, and rest yourselves under the tree".* By all means, 0 Lord allow the two with You, so a little water be brought, and wash their feet.

For this reason, our father Abraham at times talked in the singular and at other times in the plural. An example of that, if you meet an officer and two soldiers with him, you will address the conversation to the officer about himself and include the two soldiers at the same time.

As we mentioned, the three were the Lord along with two angels. The two angels went to Sodom (Gen. 19:1) and the third remained with Abraham.

It is clear that the third was the Lord and the evidences are:

He told Abraham *"I will certainly return to you according to the time of life, and behold, Sarah your wife shall have a son" (Gen. 18:10).* Furthermore the same chapter clearly indicates that He was the Lord in many verses:

* And the Lord said to Abraham, *"why did Sarah laugh" (Gen. 18:13).*

* And the Lord said *"shall I hide from Abraham what I am doing" (Gen. 18:17).*

* And the Lord said *"Because the outcry against Sodom and Gomorrah is great" (Gen. 18:20).*

Then the men turned away from there and went toward Sodom, but Abraham still stood before the Lord. *(Gen. 18:22).*

* **The saying of Abraham, *"shall not the judge of all the earth do right?"* no doubt indicates that he was talking to God as in the rest of his conversation interceding for Sodom.**
* The way Abraham put his words *"Indeed now, I who am but dust and ashes have taken it upon myself to speak to the Lord".*

* And the way the Lord put His words *"If I find in Sodom fifty righteous... I will spare all the place for their sakes" "I will not do it if I find thirty there" "I will not destroy it for the sake of ten".* It is clear those were the words of God who Has the authority to condemn and to forgive.

But the other two, were the angels that went to Sodom as it is clear from the verses *(Gen. 18:16,22)* & *(Gen. 19:1)* and their known account with Lot in *(Gen. 19)*.

The fact that the three were separated is an indication that they were not the Holy Trinity.

Two went to Sodom and the third remained with Abraham to talk to him about giving Sarah an offspring and listen to his intercession for Sodom.

This separation fits more talking about God and the two angels but not about the Trinity.

[9]

ALL WHO EVER CAME BEFORE ME ARE THIEVES AND ROBBERS

Question:

What is the meaning of the statement of the Lord *"I am the door of the sheep all who ever come before Me, are thieves and robbers, but the sheep did not hear them "* *(John 10:7-8).* **Is it believable to say about all the prophets that came before Him that they were thieves and robbers?!**

Answer:

The Lord Christ, absolutely did not mean by this statement the prophets.

Here He talked about those who did not enter from the door by saying *"I say to you, he who does not enter the sheepfold by the door, but climbs up some other way, the same is a thief and a robber" (John 10:1),* but the prophets had entered through the door and were sent by the heavenly Father.

Who are those thieves then?

They are those who came shortly before Christ, led people astray and Gamaliel talked about them.

When the chief priests brought the Apostles before them in the council, to judge them for their preaching the resurrection of the Lord, said to them *"look, you have filled Jerusalem with your doctrine, and intend to bring this Man's blood on us" (Acts 5:28); "they took council to kill them" (Acts 5:33).* Then one in the council stood up, a Pharisee named Gamaliel, a teacher of the law held in respect by all the people and commanded them to put the apostles outside, and he said to the members of the council: "Take heed to yourselves what you intend to do regarding these men."

For some time ago Theudas rose up, claiming to be somebody.

A number of men, about four hundred, joined him. He was slain, and all who obeyed him were scattered and came to nothing.

After this man, Judas of Galilee rose up in the days of the census, and drew away many people after him. He also perished, and all who obeyed him were dispersed.

And now I say to you, keep away from these men and let them alone, for if this plan or this work is of men, it will come to nothing, but if it is of God, you cannot overthrow it lest you even be found to fight against God" *(Acts 5:34-39).*

About those as Theudas and Judas of Galilee, the Lord Christ said, they were thieves and robbers.

Those that came before Him and claimed to be somebody and drew away many people after them, were dispersed.

We can add to them, those false teachers who troubled the people with their teachings and Christ called them *"blind guides"* who had the keys of the kingdom, they did not enter and prevented others from entering. *(Matt. 23:13-15).*

[10]

THE INIQUITY OF THE FATHERS ON THE CHILDREN

Question:

Could the iniquity of the fathers visit the children as the Bible says in *(Ex. 20:5)* and as we say "The fathers ate sour grapes and the children's teeth are set on edge"?

Answer:

The fathers can hand down to their children physically the result of their sins or sicknesses.

The parent could sin and as a result of his or her sin they may have contract a sickness and then the son or the daughter could inherit that sickness. The children could be stricken by mental or neurological diseases, some blood disorders or congenital defects as a result of what was inherited from their parents.

Often the sickness of the children and their suffering are a cause of pain for the parents especially if they knew that the sickness was a result of their sins.

The children might inherit ill-nature or bad character from their parents.

But this is not a rule; king Saul was cruel, merciless and of bad character. His son Jonathan was the opposite. Jonathan was a friend of David. He loved him and was faithful to him.

Even if the children inherit ill-nature from their parents, they can with ease get rid of it if they wish.

A son can inherit poverty or debts because of his father's mistakes...

He suffers because of it, of course on earth, and that would have nothing to do with his eternal life. Many are the end results that the saying of the poet agrees with (This is what my father inflicted upon me, and I did not inflict on anyone). As for judging the children for the sins that were committed personally by their parents, the Bible has refuted completely as written in he Book of Ezekiel "what do you mean when you use this proverb... the fathers have eaten sour grapes, and the children's teeth are set on edge? 'As I live' says the Lord God, you shall no longer use this proverb the soul who sins shall die... "

The son shall not bear the guilt of the father, nor the father bear the guilt of the son:

"The righteousness of the righteous shall be upon himself, and the wickedness of the wicked shall be upon himself. (Ezek. 18:1-20).

The righteous Jonathan did not bear the evil of his father king Saul nor Josiah the righteous king the sin of Aaron his father or Manasseh his grandfather or the rest of his forefathers.

The curses of the law in the Old Testament was abolished in the New Testament. As we say in the Anaphora of St. Gregory:

[You have lifted the curse of the Law].

As an example of this curse, Canaan, did bear the curse of his father Ham, *(Gen. 9:22-25)* and his sons also bore it till the days of the Lord Christ and not only till the fourth generation.

Now, we are in the era of *"grace and truth" (John 1:17)* so do not be afraid of the curse of the Law which was inherited by the children from their grandfathers.

Often the father could be evil but the son is righteous refusing to walk in his father's footsteps, and even he might resist him as the Lord says, *"He who loves father or mother more than Me is not worthy of Me." (Matt. 10:37).*

Naturally it would be unjust for God to visit the sins of this evil father on his righteous son who deserves to be rewarded.

[11]

THE COMMENDATION OF THE UNJUST STEWARD

Question:

The Bible says *"So the Master commended the unjust steward" (Luke 16:8).* How did the Lord commend the unjust steward?

Answer:

The Lord did not commend all his actions, He only commended his wisdom.

The conclusion of this verse says *"so the master commended the unjust steward because he had done wisely".* This man was prepared for whatever the future might bring him before he was discharged from his stewardship. This readiness in this parable symbolises the readiness that we should have toward eternity before we depart from this world.

The Lord, by this parable admonishes us by the wisdom which the people of the world have.
So if the people of this world in spite of their sins, have such wisdom then the sons of God should also have it. For immediately after praising the unjust steward on his wisdom

He said, *'for the sons of this world are more shrewd in their generation than the sons of light" (Luke 16:8)*. The Lord is reproaching us by the parable of the unjust steward who being a son of this world, knew how to be ready for his future.

We need to bring up an important point in this parable and other parables like it:

There is a specific point of comparison, not a generalised one.

For example if we praise the lion, we do not praise its savageness and wildness but we praise its strength and courage. If we describe a man as a lion we do not mean that he is an animal or a savage but we praise him for his strength and courage. Also in the parable of the unjust steward the praise was for one specific point only which is the wisdom of being ready for the future, not his other qualities.

Here we give another example to clarify this point: The serpent, which is the cause of the calamity and fall of the human race, the Lord found a nice thing about it that we might adopt, He said:

"Be wise as serpents... " (Matt. 10:16)
Does that mean that we should be like the serpent in every thing? While it is a symbol of wickedness, evil and cunning. The only point that God praised in the serpent is the wisdom, so the resemblance is only limited to this quality, as with the unjust steward.

[12]

"THIS GENERATION PASSED AWAY"

Question:

The Lord Christ in chapter 24 of the gospel of St. Matthew talked about the signs of the time and the end of the age saying *" Assuredly, I say to you, this generation will by no means pass away till all these things take place " (Matt. 24:34).* This generation had passed and many other generations after it and the world did not end ... ! How can we explain that'?

Answer:

In fact the Lord Christ in *(Matt. 24)* and also in *(Mark 13)* was talking about two subjects: the destruction of Jerusalem and the end of the world and not about the latter only.

His saying *"this generation will by no means pass away till all these things are fulfilled"* meant the realisation of His prophecy regarding the destruction of Jerusalem. This was fulfilled when Jerusalem was destroyed in the year 70 AD and the Jews were dispersed all over the earth and that generation was still around.

Other prophecies of the Lord Christ in this chapter regarding the destruction of Jerusalem, not the end of the world are as follows:

+ *"Matt. 24:15-20 "Therefore when you see the 'abomination of desolation,' spoken of by Daniel the prophet, standing in the holy place"* (whoever reads, let him understand), *"then let those who are in Judea flee to the mountains. "Let him who is on the housetop not go down to take anything out of his house. "And let him who is in the field not go back to get his clothes. "But woe to those who are pregnant and to those who are nursing babies in those days! "And pray that your flight may not be in winter or on the Sabbath."*

+ *" Then they will deliver you up to tribulation and kill you, and you will be hated by all nations for My name's sake. "And then many will be offended, will betray one another..." (Matt. 24:9-10).*

+ *"Then two men will be in the field: one will be taken and the other left. "Two women will be grinding at the mill: one will be taken and the other left. " (Matt. 24:40-41)*

Therefore, do not take the whole chapter as prophecies about the end of the world.

The phrase *"the coming of the Son of Man "* means the second coming at the end of the age and it also means His coming as far as the life of every human, as He said *"Blessed are those servants whom the master, when he comes, will find watching... therefore you also be ready, for the Son of Man is coming at an hour you do not except... blessed is that servant whom his master will find so doing when he comes" (Luke 12:37,40,43).* Also *"lest, coming suddenly He find you sleeping" (Mark 13:36).*

[13]

THE BLASPHEMY AGAINST THE HOLY SPIRIT

Question:

The verse that says *"Therefore I say to you, every sin and blasphemy will be forgiven men, but the blasphemy against the Spirit will not be forgiven "* (Matt. 12:31) alarm me very much. Sometimes I think that I committed the sin of blasphemy so I fall into despair. Please explain the meaning of the blasphemy against the Holy Spirit? And how is that there is no forgiveness either in this age or in the age to come? How does this unforgiveness coincide with the mercy of God and His many promises?

Answer:

All your fears are temptations from the devil to make you fall into despair so be comforted.

As for the meaning of the blasphemy against the Spirit and the sin that is without forgiveness, this, with the grace of God I shall explain to you.

The blasphemy against the Holy Spirit is not the unbelief in the Holy Spirit or His Divinity or His work and it is not insulting of the Holy Spirit. If the atheists believe, God forgives them for their unbelief and their mockery of God and His Holy Spirit. All those who followed Macedonius in his heresy and his denial of the Divinity of the Holy Spirit, when repented the church accepted, them and forgave them.

What then is the blasphemy against the Holy Spirit? And why there is no forgiveness for it?

The blasphemy against the Holy Spirit is the complete and continuous refusal of any work of the Spirit in the heart which is a life time refusal.

As a result of this refusal, man does not repent and accordingly God does not forgive him.

God in His mercy accepts every repentance and forgives as He said, *"The one who comes to Me I will by no means cast out" (John 6:37)* and the saints were correct in their saying: *"All that the Father gives Me will come to Me, and the one who comes to Me I will by no means cast out".*

[There is no sin without forgiveness except that without repentance].

So if a person dies in his sin without repentance, he will perish as the Lord said *"Unless you repent you will all likewise perish " (Luke 13:5).*

Then non repentance till death is the only sin that is without forgiveness. If the matter is so, that brings up a question:

What is the relation between lack of repentance and the blasphemy against the Holy Spirit?

Obviously, a person cannot repent without the work of the Spirit in him. For the Holy Spirit will reprove the world of sin *(John 16:8)* and lead the person in the spiritual life and encourage him. He is the power that aids in every good work.

Without the communion of the Holy Spirit, no one can accomplish any spiritual work.

So the refusal of the communion of the Holy Spirit *(2 Cor 13:14)* absolutely can not produce any good. For all the works of righteousness the apostle had put under the title *"fruit of the Spirit" (GaL 5:22)*. That person without any fruit will be cut down and thrown into the fire *(Matt. 3:10)* & *(John 15:4-5)*.

He who refuses the Spirit, will not repent, and will not bring forth any spiritual fruit.

If his refusal of the Spirit is a complete and life long refusal, then he will spend all his life without repentance, without works of righteousness and without fruit of the Spirit, so of course he will perish. This is the blasphemy against the Holy Spirit.

It is not that the person grieves the Spirit *(Eph. 4:30)* or quenches the Spirit *(1Thess. 5:19)* or resists the Spirit *(Acts 7:51)* but it is the complete and persistent refusal of the Spirit. So he would not repent and would not have fruits in a righteous life.

Here we are faced with a question:

What if a person refuses all works of the Spirit then turns back and accepts Him and repents?

We say that his repentance and acceptance of the Spirit even just before the end of his life, is an indication that the Spirit of God still works in him and led him to repentance. Then his refusal of the Spirit was not complete and not life long. A case like this is not a blasphemy against the Holy Spirit according to the definition mentioned before.

To fall into a sin that has no forgiveness is a form of a war of the devil against us to make us fall into despair which will destroy us, make us depressed; and that does not help us in any spiritual work.

To the person that asked the question I say: the mere asking of the question is an indication of your concern about eternal fate. This is not blasphemy against the Spirit.

Now we need to answer the last part of the question.

How this unforgiveness coincides with the mercy of God?

God is always ready to forgive and nothing prevents His forgiveness, but the important thing is that the person repents to deserve forgiveness.

If the person refuses repentance, God waits for his repentance till the uttermost breath of his life, as happened with the thief at the Lord's right hand. If the person refuses to repent all his life and refuses the work of the Spirit in him till the time of his death then he not God-blessed be His name would be responsible for the perishing of his soul.

[14]

WHAT IS THE BOOK OF JASHER?

Question:

What is the book of Jasher? Is it one of the Books of the Holy Bible or the Torah (Pentateuch)? How was it mentioned in the Book of Joshua and in the Book of 2 Samuel and yet it is not part of the Bible?

Answer:

The word "book" could mean any book; religious or secular.

The book of Jasher is an old secular book which included the popular songs, that were in circulation among the Jews, which were based on important religious and secular events. Some of these songs were military songs for the soldiers.

This book dates back to 1000-800 BC, more than 500 years after Moses the Prophet. It contained things pertaining to David the Prophet and his lamentation for king Saul.

It is not part of the Torah (Pentateuch) of Moses, for it included events that happened many centuries after Moses.

People chanted some of the important historical events of the olden times, and wrote hymns about these events and gathered them in this book which grew by time and had nothing to do with the Divine inspiration.

An example is: The battle of Gideon during the days of Joshua, where the sun stood still. The people wrote songs about this. These were added on to the book of Jasher. Joshua referred to them saying *"Is this not written in the book of Jasher" (Josh. 10:13),* which meant isn't this one of the important current events, that because of its fame, popular songs were written about, in secular books as the book of Jasher.

Also, the beautiful and moving song, by which David mourned king Saul and his son Jonathan, the people admired and chanted it. They included it in their popular secular books, since it concerned the killing of their first king along with the successor to his throne. So when this event was told in the Book of 2nd Samuel, it was said about it *"indeed it is written in the book of Jasher" (2 Sam. 1:17)* which meant that the lamentation of David became a popular song, the people added it to their book of hymns known as the Book of Jasher. **This is exactly as we speak about a famous event that is mentioned in the Holy Bible as it is also mentioned in the history books.**

Finally: did the Jews omit it from the Torah (the Pentateuch) for a religious reason? and the answer is clear:

A. It is not part of the Torah. For the Torah is the five Books of Moses which are Genesis, Exodus, Leviticus, Numbers and Deuteronomy.

B. If the Jews wanted to hide it for a religious reason, they would not mention it in the Book of Joshua and the Book of Samuel the Prophet.

C. The oldest and most famous translation of the Old Testament which is the Septuagint that was written in the third century BC does not include this book.

[15]

THE APPEARANCE OF THE LORD TO SAUL

Question:

There are two accounts in the Book of the Acts of the Apostles about the appearance of the Lord to Saul. It seems that there are some contradictions between both accounts, in what they saw or heard, please explain.

Answer:

The account of the appearance of the Lord to Saul recorded in the ninth chapter, verse 7 states *"And the men who journeyed with him stood speechless, hearing a voice but seeing no one."* The same incident also described in the twenty second chapter, verse 9 states *"Now those who were with me indeed saw the light and were afraid, but they did not hear the voice of Him who spoke to me."*

The key to this problem, is that the men who accompanied St. Paul were not on the same spiritual level to see what he saw and to hear what he heard.

This vision was not for them, the apparition of the Lord was not for them and the conversation of the Lord was not with them, but that all was only for Saul of Tarsus.

Nevertheless, there is no contradiction between the two accounts as far as what the men heard or saw as we closely examine both stories, we realise that **the men who accompanied Saul, heard his voice talking to the Lord, but they did not hear the voice of the Lord when He talked to Saul.**

So if we read the two statements carefully, we realise what proves that, without any contradiction:

1. Hearing a voice but seeing no one.

2. They saw the light but they did not hear the voice of Him who spoke to Paul.

The voice that is mentioned in the first statement, is the voice of Saul. They heard him talking without seeing with whom he talked. The voice that they couldn't hear is that of the one talking to Saul. **Then there is no contradiction as far as the voice is concerned**.

It could have been contradicting, if it had been said in the first statement "They heard the voice of he who spoke to me" or "heard what I heard", but the word (voice) only meant here the voice of Saul for the spiritual level of those men is to hear the voice of a man but not the voice of the Lord.

The same applies to the vision also: **They saw the light, but they did not see the person who was talking to Saul**. This is clear from the way the two statements were put:

1. seeing no one *(Acts 9:7)*.

2. Saw the light and were afraid *(Acts 22:9)*.

The light is one thing but the face and shape of the person that was talking is another.

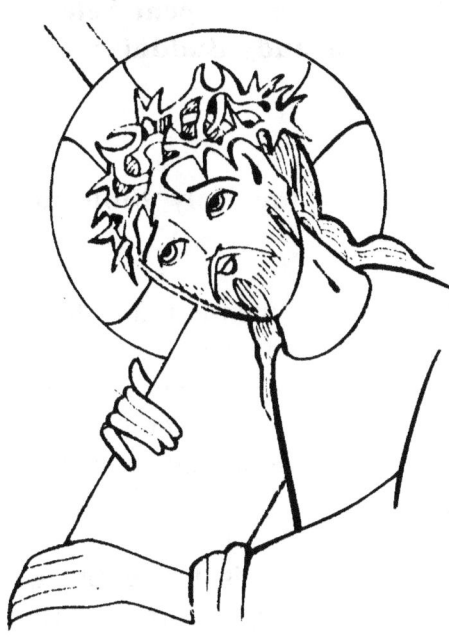

[16]

CHRIST BEFORE THE THIRTIETH

Question:

Why did the Bible not mention the biography of the thirty years the Lord Christ spent before His ministry? Did He go to China to study Buddhism as some say?

Answer:

It was not meant for the Holy Bible to be a book of history.

If the Gospels were to mention all the events and the historical details *"even the world itself could not contain the books that would be written" (John 21:25)*. The details of one day in the life of the Lord Christ on earth with all the teachings and miracles would alone need more than one book.

The intent of the Gospel is to be the good tidings of salvation, telling the history of our salvation.

Therefore the Gospels started by the miraculous birth of Christ from a Virgin, the angels involved in the story of the Divine birth, also the genealogy of Christ, and the fulfilment of the prophecies pertaining to His birth. Then they moved on to His baptism and the start of His ministry. As an example of His childhood, His meeting with the elders of the Jews and their astonishment of His answers *(Luke 2:46)*... was mentioned to point out His teaching abilities since His young age.

But the claim that He went to China is unfounded.

This claim has no support from the Bible history or tradition. Those who say that are anti-Christ whose purpose is to mislead the people that Christ took His teachings from Buddhism. Therefore it was proper for the Gospel to mention the surpassing knowledge of Christ since His young age so that the elders were astonished by His answers. He did not need to go to China or elsewhere.

The teachings of the Lord Christ are superior to Buddhism and to any other teaching.

Any learner can discover this unmeasurable superiority. It is not the place here to compare, but if there were a resemblance between His teaching and Buddhism, the Buddhists would have believed in Him.

The magnificence of the Lord Christ is not confined only to His teaching. Did He also take His majestic miracles from Buddhism?!

Did He take from Buddhism the raising of the dead, opening the eyes of the blind, the rebuking of the sea, walking on water, the feeding of the multitudes, healing the incurable diseases, casting out demons and the other countless miracles.

Did He take from Buddhism the Salvation that He offered to the world?

We should not let our imagination run about the thirty years prior to His ministry. It is enough to know that the Lord Christ started His public ministry according to the Law *(Num. 4:3, 23 & 47; 1 Chr. 23:3)* when He was thirty.

What we need to know about the story of Salvation is the ministry of Christ after His thirtieth year, added to that His Virginal birth and all the prophecies and miracles around it.

[17]

LITTLE OF WINE

Question:

Is there a verse in the Bible that says *"A little wine is good for the stomach"*. Does this verse encourage the drinking of alcoholic beverages?

Answer:

There is no verse in the Bible with this wording, but this is a common distorted saying among the people.

St. Timothy, the bishop and disciple of St. Paul the apostle, suffered from many ailments in his digestive system, and it was also said that he had dropsy. The apostle prescribed to him not to drink much water and to take; as a treatment for his special condition; a little wine, so he said to him *"No longer drink only water, but use a little wine for your stomach's sake and your frequent infirmities." (1 Tim. 5:23).*

We notice here that we have a specific patient, who has a particular disease, needs a special treatment suitable for his condition in a time medical sciences had not developed as it is nowadays and at that time wine was used as medicine.

Then the Bible did not give a general ruling that a little of wine is good for the stomach but the apostle gave a treatment for a specific condition.

So if you had the same condition as Timothy and were in the same time, this advice would be suitable for you. Nowadays, even if you have the same disease of St. Timothy medical sciences will offer you the most recent advances in remedies.

Notice, in the parable of the good Samaritan, that when he found a wounded man by the road, *"he bandaged his wounds, pouring on oil and wine" (Luke 10:34).* The alcohol in the wine was used as an antiseptic to control bleeding.

So all what we understand from the advice that was given to St. Timothy is that:

The wine was prescribed as a treatment and not as a pleasure and only for a special case.

This is also a matter of conscience; does every one who partake of it now, take it only as a treatment and has no other suitable treatment except it?

We are speaking about wine as a treatment. The subject of wine and alcoholic beverages in detail is not the question.

[18]

THE POTTER AND THE CLAY

Question:

Don't we say that man is free to choose? Then why are these verses mentioned in the Bible: *" But indeed, O man, who are you to reply against God? Will the thing formed say to him who formed it, "Why have you made me like this?" Does not the potter have power over the clay, from the same lump to make one vessel for honour and another for dishonour? "(Rom. 9:20-21)*

Was it my fault then, if the potter made me a vessel of dishonour?!

Answer:

Yes, the potter has power over the clay to make of it what he desires, a vessel for honour or a vessel of dishonour and the clay cannot say "Why did you make me like this?".

But the potter also is wise and just.

One of the wonderful explanations that I read about this subject:

That the potter, with all his freedom and authority, wisely looked at the piece of day. If he found it good, soft and smooth, he would make of it a vessel for honour; for its quality qualifies it for that.

It is illogical that a wise potter with a piece of high quality clay, will make of it a vessel of dishonour, that would be carelessness, far be it from God to do so!

If the clay was rough and of poor quality and not fit to be a vessel for honour, the potter, because of the clay condition, would make of it a vessel of dishonour.

With all possibilities, he will try to make of the clay, all the clay in front of him, vessels of honour as far as the quality of the clay allows it.

Then, after all, it depends on the quality of the clay and how good it is, recognising the authority of the potter and his freedom adding to that this wisdom and justice. Therefore God said " *Look, as the clay is in the potter's hand, so are you in My hand, O house of Israel! "The instant I speak concerning a nation and concerning a kingdom, to pluck up, to pull down, and to destroy it, "if that nation against whom I have spoken turns from its evil, I will relent of the disaster that I thought to bring upon it. "And the instant I speak concerning a nation and concerning a kingdom, to build and to plant it, "if it does evil in My sight so that it does not obey My voice, then I will relent concerning the good with which I said I would* *benefit it." (Jer. 18:6-10).* Then the clay has the chance to improve or change its fate.

This reminds us of the parable of the sower that went out to sow *(Matt. 13:3-8).*

The sower is the same as the seeds are the same and the sower wishes all to grow, but according to the nature of the earth on which the seeds fell, was the result, growing or spoiling. The sower did not prepare the seeds to be devoured by birds, or wither away or be choked by the thorns but the nature of the earth controlled that.

Do not say then, "was it my fault that I became a vessel of dishonour?!"

Be a good and soft clay in the hand of the great potter and be assured that He will make of you a vessel of honour, and the matter is still in your hand.

[19]

IS THIS METEMPHSYCHOSIS?

Question:

What does the Bible mean by saying that John the Baptist came in the spirit and power of Elijah *(Luke 1:17)*, and its saying: he is Elijah who is to come. *(Matt. 11:14)*. Is this metempsychosis (reincarnation)? Did the spirit of Elijah reincarnate in John?

Answer:

The coming of John in the spirit of Elijah, means he came with the same style of Elijah, his manner, his method and his spirit of doing things.

1. Elijah was ascetic, and also was John the Baptist. Elijah *"was a hairy man, and wore a leather belt around his waist" (2 Kin. 1:8),* and John *"himself was clothed in camel's hair, with a leather belt around his waist" (Matt. 3:4).* They both had the same look and same clothes.

Elijah lived in the wilderness, on Mount Carmel *(1 Kin. 18:19 & 24),* in a cave on Horeb, the mountain of God *(1 Kin. 18:9),* in an upper room *(1 Kin. 17:19)* or at the brook cherish *(1 Kin. 1 7:3)* and John the Baptist was in the wilderness *(Matt. 3:1; Luke 3:2)* and then beside the Jordan river. He was the voice of one crying in the wilderness *(Mark 1:3).*

2. Elijah started with the life of solitude and contemplation and the Lord chose him for ministry and prophecy. John also lived the life of solitude in the wilderness; then started preaching repentance.

3. Elijah was courageous and firm in the truth. He killed the prophets of Baal *(1 Kin 18:40),* and also said *" And fire came down from heaven and consumed him and his fifty." (2 Kin. 1:10).* John the Baptist was harsh in admonishing the sinners. He used to say, *"And even now the axe is laid to the root of the trees. Therefore every tree which does not bear good fruit is cut down and thrown into the fire " (Luke 3:9).*

4. Elijah rebuked king Ahab and told him, *"Is that you, 0 troubler of Israel?... but you and your father's house have, in that you have forsaken the commandments of the LORD and have followed the Baals " (1 Kin. 18:18).* He also rebuked and warned him for the slaying of Naboth the Jezreelite *(1 Kin. 21:20-29),* and he also vowed the punishment of queen Jezebel.

John the Baptist rebuked king Herod saying, *"It is not lawful for you to have your brother's wife" (Mark 6:18).*

Then John was acting with the same spirit as Elijah and his method.

Elisha requested from his teacher Elijah before he was taken away to heaven, *"Let a double portion of your spirit be upon me" (1 Kin. 2:9)* and it was. So when Elisha performed miracles with the same strength as Elijah and the sons of the prophets saw him they said, *"The spirit of Elijah rests on Elisha and they came to meet him, and bowed to the ground before him." (2 Kin. 2:14-15)*.

If the matter is transmigration of souls, what is the meaning of the phrase *"double portion of Elijah's spirit"*. Did Elijah have two spirits? Did his spirit reincarnate in Elisha before it was reincarnated in John?!

It was a double strength, double the power that was in Elijah, that came down upon Elisha and the same power was in John.

When the apostle said, *" endeavouring to keep the unity of the Spirit in the bond of peace. There is one body and one Spirit, just as you were called in one hope of your calling " (Eph. 4:3-4)*, he did not mean literally that we all should have one spirit or one body but the same course, way, and style. The same meaning about the phrase, *"One heart and one soul"*, that was said about those who believed in the apostolic age. *(Acts 4:32)*

Christianity does not believe in the reincarnation of the spirits.

When the spirit leaves a body, it does not return again to this body or to any other body. If it is righteous it goes to

Paradise as the spirit of the thief, but if it is evil it goes to Hades as the spirit of the rich man while Lazarus' spirit went to Paradise.

You find reincarnation in a religion like Brahmanism or in a philosophy like Plutonism.

The Brahmans believe that the soul transmigrates from one body to another and these reincarnations represent punishment or reward for that spirit. The spirit goes on like this until it is freed to the upper space. This condition is called "Nirvana" which is reached by much asceticism.

As for Plato, he saw that the number of spirits were limited so that it was necessary for the spirits to transmigrate from one body to another.

These beliefs and religions have no relation to Christianity.

[20]

ABOUT THE MEANING OF THE "MAMMON OF UNRIGHTEOUSNESS"

Question:

What is the meaning of the saying of the Lord Christ *"Make friends for yourselves by unrighteous mammon " (Luke 16:9)?* Can the money that we gain by injustice or through sin in general, be accepted by God, or can we use it to do good, or to win friends with it?

Answer:

"Mammon of Unrighteousness" does not mean the illicit money that the person gains unjustly or through any other sin for that is unacceptable to God.

For God and the church do not accept this money.

The psalm said *"The oil of the sinner will not anoint my head",* and in Deuteronomy *"You shall not bring the wages of a harlot... to the house of the Lord your God" (Deut. 23:18).*

God does not accept the good works that come through evil ways.

The oblations that are offered to the church, bring blessings and are mentioned in the litany of crops and in the litany of oblations before God. Therefore there are rejected offerings which the church does not accept and does not allow in the house of the Lord, if the church knows that it came by wrong means, and the canon of the apostles explained that subject.

Then what is the mammon of unrighteousness by which we should make friends?

The mammon of unrighteousness is not the money that you gain unjustly but the money that you keep unjustly.

What does that mean? When would the money be called so? Here is an example:

God gave you money, with it He gave you the commandment of paying tithes. Then the tithes does not belong to you. It belongs to the Lord, the church, and the poor. If you do not pay it, you are being unjust to those who deserve it, and by keeping this money you are stealing from them. **This tithes that you did not give to their rightful owners is mammon of unrighteousness you are keeping.**

The Lord says in the Book of Malachi the Prophet " *Will a man rob God? Yet you have robbed Me! But you say, 'In what way have we robbed You?' In tithes and offerings* ". *(Mal. 3:8)*.

So if you keep the tithes, the first fruits and the votive offerings, you will be unjust to the poor, orphan, and the widow, and they are all crying to the Lord for your injustice towards them.

Spending this money for your own purposes entails injustice to the house of God. This money belongs to God and His children and is not yours.

We can say that also about all the idle wealth that you might have and in the mean time the poor need it and they are in trouble because of their need.

Then make friends to your self by this mammon of unrighteousness. Give it to those in need of it, satisfy their needs. They will become your friends and pray for you and the Lord will respond and bless your money and you will be rewarded more and more.

[21]

WHY FORGIVE THEM?

Question:

Why did our Lord Jesus Christ say on the cross *"Father, forgive them... " (Luke 23:34)* **and did not say by His own authority** *"your sins are forgiven...*

Answer:

The Lord Christ on the cross was representing all mankind.

He represented all humanity in paying the wages of sin to the Divine Justice... *" All we like sheep have gone astray; We have turned, every one, to his own way; And the LORD has laid on Him the iniquity of us all." (Is. 53:6).* For this reason, He was on the cross *"a burnt sacrifice... a sweet aroma unto the Lord" (Lev. 1:9),* and He was a sin offering, and also a *"Passover" (1 Cor. 5:7).*

He was offering to the Father an atonement for our sins, and as He offered this sacrifice, He said to the Father *"forgive them".*

In other words: "I have satisfied the Justice that You, O Father, have demanded, and therefore, forgive them".

I have paid the wages of sin and shed My blood to redeem them, therefore forgive them". He spoke as an advocate on behalf of all humanity before the Father, as a representative of every sinner from Adam until the end of all ages.

In His intercession, He was announcing His abdication of His rights toward His crucifiers, those who insulted Him without reason, condemned Him to die unjustly, who falsely accused Him, and stirred the crowd against Him without knowing what they were doing.

He said that as a representative on their behalf as an intercessor for them on the cross.

However, in other circumstances, He performed the forgiveness by Himself as God. He said to the sick man with palsy *"Your sins are forgiven" (Mark 2:5)* giving the evidence of His Divinity and His authority to forgive sins. Also He said to the sinful woman in the house of Simon the Pharisee *"Your sins are forgiven. " (Luke 7:48)*. His authority to forgive sins did not depart from Him on the cross, for He forgave the thief on His right, and said to him *"Today you will be with Me in Paradise" (Luke 23:43)* declaring His forgiveness of his sins, without which he could not enter Paradise.

[22]

THE MEANING OF CERTAIN WORDS

Question:

We read in the Bible some words which need to be translated or explained in simple terms, as in the following:

Selah : Which is mentioned quite often in the psalms, as in *Psalms 46 to 50.*

Maran-a'tha : mentioned in *(1 Cor. 16:22).*

Anathema : mentioned in *(Gal. 1:8-9)* and *(1 Cor. 16:22).*

Kedar : as in *(Ps. 120:5)* and *(Song. 1:5).*

Please explain the meaning of these words, so that we may understand them.

Answer:

SELAH

It is a word that is repeated in the Psalms 71 times. It means a musical stop to change the tune to another, for the psalms were sung associated with music at the time of

David, Asaph and others. At a certain place of the song, a sign was given to stop to give a chance to the musicians to adjust their musical instruments to a new tune.

MARAN-A'THA

The word "Mar", in Syrian and Aramaic means Master or Lord.

The word 'a'tha' means come.

The whole word means "the Lord comes" or "the Lord will come".

It was an expression that Christians used to greet each other with during the apostolic age, comforting each other with the coming of the Lord. In other words, they say to each other "rejoice, the Lord is coming again".

Sometimes, they wrote it at the end of their letters, as St. Paul concluded his first epistle to the Corinthians.

ANATHEMA

It is a Greek word that means "curse", and it also means the "cutting off" or the excommunication from the church. As in the Anathemas that were written by St. Kyrollos (Cyril) the pillar of faith during the heresy of Nestor upon every one who would violate the canons of faith.

St. Paul used it in his epistle to the Galatians to excommunicate by his ecclesiastical authority everyone who taught against the teaching of the apostles, even if it was an angel, he said *"But even if we, or an angel from heaven, preach any other gospel to you than what we have preached to you, let him be accursed.(anathema). " (Gal. 1:8)*. He used the same statement at the end of his first epistle to the Corinthians. This statement is very well known in the church canons.

KEDAR

Kedar is the second son of Ishmael, the son of Hagar *(Gen. 25:13)*. The area where he lived was called after his name also *(Jer. 49:28)*. The children of Kedar lived in tents that were black in colour or looked black because of the smoke of the fire that warmed them at night. Perhaps this is what the virgin of the Song of songs meant when she said *"I am dark, but lovely, 0 daughters of Jerusalem, like the tents of Kedar... " (Song. 1:5)*. The psalmist mentioned *"the tents of Kedar"* as a sojourn country *(Ps. 120:5)*.

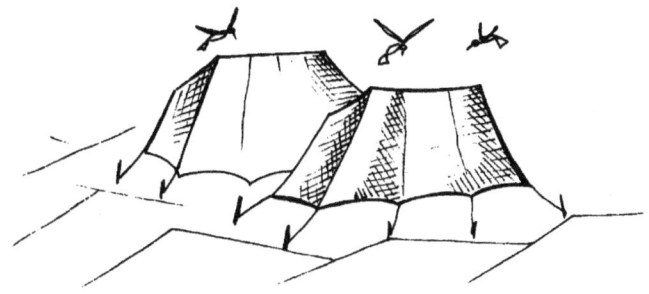

[23]

THE RICH AND ENTERING THE KINGDOM

Question:

The Lord said: *"It is easier for a camel to go through the eye of a needle than for a rich man to enter the kingdom of God."* **(Mark 10:25)**

Does this mean that all the rich cannot enter the kingdom?

Answer:

No, for some rich people are righteous and saintly.

The Lord made this statement as a comment on the conduct of the rich young man whose riches hindered him from following the Lord. He went away grieved for he had great possessions.

The Lord did not say that the entrance of the rich into the kingdom was impossible but He said it was hard. He did not mention all the rich but He said: *"Children, how hard it is for those who trust in riches to enter the kingdom of God!"* *(Mark 10:24).*

Therefore, there is a specific shortcoming, which is the dependence on money not on God. This shortcoming then develops from depending on money, to the love of money and its worship, to being a competitor against God. The Lord said *"No one can serve two masters.. You cannot serve God and mammon" (Matt. 6:24).*

Those who allow money to compete with God in their hearts will find it difficult to enter the kingdom.

This is exactly what happened with this young rich man. He could observe all the commandments from his youth, except his love for money, for it was indispensable to him.

There is also another flaw that can prevent the rich from entering the kingdom and that is **the stinginess in spending money and consequently the cruelty of the heart toward the poor.**

An example for this is the rich man who lived at the time of Lazarus the beggar who desired to be fed with the crumbs which fell from the rich man's table. The rich man did not have any pity toward this beggar, for in his cruelty of heart, he left the dogs to lick his sores. *(Luke 16:19-21).*

In spite of all that the rich can be saved and enter into the kingdom.

The rich that owns the money and does not allow the money to own him. He owns the money, but does not allow the love of money to enter his heart to prevent him to love God and the neighbour. He spends his money in charitable acts.

The Bible gives us examples for saintly rich people like Job the Righteous...

Job was the richest man in the east in his days, and the Bible gives us a detailed account of his wealth before his trial *(Job 1:2 & 3)* and after *(Job 42:12)*. The Lord Himself testified for Job saying: *"There is none like him on the earth, a blameless and upright man, one who fears God and shuns evil" (Job 1:8)*. He gave to the poor, he was as father to them, and he caused the widow's heart to sing for joy, he was eyes to the blind, and he was feet to the lame. He delivered the poor who cried out and he who had no helper. *(Job 29:12-16)*.

The Lord blessed Job's wealth after the tribulation and doubled it.

For the wealth in his hand was a tool for the good and also for the building of the kingdom.

Also the Patriarchs Abraham, Isaac and Jacob, were very rich in their times. Abraham was like a king who could defeat four kings, and was received by kings upon his return from the battle *(Gen. 14)*. He was generous and had great love for God and for people. In the other world, Abraham had a great gulf fixed between him and the rich man in the Lazarus parable *(Luke 16:26)*. This scene gives us the difference between two rich people, one in bliss, and the other in torment.

The gospel gives us another example of a holy rich man as Abraham, that is, Joseph from Arimathea.

St. Joseph of Arimathea was worthy to take the body of Jesus to wrap and bury it in his new tomb. It was said about him that he was a rich man *(Matt. 27:57)* and in spite of that he was waiting for the kingdom of God *(Mark 15:43)*. The Gospel of St. Luke said about him that he was *"A council member, a good and just man." (Luke 23:50)* Joseph of Arimathea was one of the rich men who entered the kingdom.

We should also mention the righteous rich people who lived during the apostolic age.

The Book of Acts says about them: *" Nor was there anyone among them who lacked; for all who were possessors of lands or houses sold them, and brought the proceeds of the things that were sold, and laid them at the apostles' feet; and they distributed to each as anyone had need. (Acts 4:34-35)*. An example of these people was Joseph who was also named Barnabas by the apostles *(Acts 4:36-37)*. He was the one that the Holy Spirit chose to serve with St. Paul *(Acts 13:2)*.

History also gives us other examples of holy rich people who entered the kingdom of God.

St. Melania, who was very rich, spent much of her money on monasteries and on building churches. She then chose the monastic life after she was widowed.

St. Paula, who sponsored St. Jerome and his monastic life, built a monastery and a convent in Palestine. She became the abbess of that convent after her widowhood. Her daughter "Yustokhiom" became the superior after her departure.

Another example for these righteous rich people is **"Ibrahim El-Gouhary"** who spent his money on maintaining churches, monks, monasteries and the construction of holy places.

Wealth is not a hindrance toward the kingdom, but the hindrance is the heart...

The problem is: that the heart surrenders to the love of wealth, and it becomes a burden to give even the tithes and gather money without a certain goal in mind, and money becomes an idol that he worships, which becomes a hindrance to the love of God.

The rich man who uses his money in charitable acts in sacrificial love is not the rich man that our Lord Jesus Christ described.

A reference to this subject is a book written by St. Clement of Alexandria. He was the dean of the school of Alexandria who preceded Origen. The name of the book is "The rich man who can be saved". This book has been translated by father Mousa Wahba, and is recommended for reading.

[24]

WHICH HEAVEN DID THEY ASCEND TO?

Question:

It was said about Enoch that he ascended to heaven *(Gen. 5:24),* and the same was said about Elijah the prophet *(2 Kin. 2:11).* St. Paul also said that he was caught up to the third heaven, whether in the body or out of the body, he did not know *(2 Cor. 12:2).*

How then did our Lord Jesus Christ say to Nicodemus: *" No one has ascended to heaven but He who came down from heaven, that is, the Son of Man who is in heaven." (John 3:13)?* Did not Enoch and Elijah ascend to heaven?

Also, what is the third heaven? and how many heavens are there in the Bible?

Answer:

The heaven that the Lord descended from and again ascended to is not the same heaven that Enoch and Elijah ascended to.

The heavens that we know of which the Bible mentioned are:

1. The heavens of the birds. The heaven where birds fly is the atmosphere that surrounds us. The Bible mentions the birds of the air *(Gen. 1:26)* and *(Gen. 7:3)*. This heaven has the clouds which carry rain *(Gen. 8:2)* and where aeroplanes now fly, whether below or above.

2. The second heaven, is higher than the heaven of the birds. It is the heaven of the sun, the moon and stars. In other words the firmament as it was called by God: *"And God called the firmament Heaven " (Gen. 1:8).*

The Bible says *"The stars of heaven" (Mark 13:25),* and God said about it: *"Let there be lights in the firmament of the heavens... to give light on the earth... then God made two great lights... and the stars" (Gen. 1:14-17).* This heaven is different from the heaven of the birds. This heaven will pass away on the last day *"Heaven and earth pass away" (Matt. 5:18)* and as St. John said in Revelation: *"And I saw a new heaven and a new earth, for the first heaven and the first earth has passed away. Also there was no more sea" (Rev. 21:1).*

3. The third heaven is Paradise.

That was the heaven that St. Paul ascended to, and said about himself: *"Such a one was caught up to the third heaven... he was caught up into Paradise" (2 Col. 12:2-4).*

It is the same heaven about which the Lord said to the thief on His right: *"You will be with Me in Paradise" (Luke 23:43).* It is the same place to which the Lord relocated the spirits of the righteous people of the Old Testament, who waited on the hope of salvation and to which the spirits of the righteous ascend now till the day of resurrection when all will be moved to the heavenly Jerusalem *(Rev. 21)*.

4. The heaven of heavens, is above and beyond all the previously mentioned heavens.

The psalmist said about it: *"Praise Him, you heavens of heavens" (Ps. 148:4).* This is the heaven about which the Lord said: *"No one has ascended to heaven but He who came down from heaven, that is, the Son of Man who is in heaven. (John 3:13).*

It is the heaven where the throne of God is.

The psalmist said about it: *"The Lord's throne is in heaven;" (Ps. 11:4; 103:19). The Lord commanded us not to swear by heaven, for it is God's throne (Matt. 5:34).* This is what is mentioned in (Isaiah 66:1) and what St. Stephen also saw during his stoning: *"I saw the heavens opened and the Son of man standing at the right hand of God. " (Acts 7:55 & 56).*

All the heavens that humans have reached, are nothing compared to the heaven of heavens. For this reason, it was said about our Lord: *"Has passed through the heavens" (Heb. 4:14), "And has become higher than the heavens" (Heb. 7:26).*

Solomon the Wise mentioned the heaven of heavens on the day he consecrated the temple. He said to the Lord in his prayer: *"Behold, heaven and the heaven of heavens cannot contain You" (1 Kin. 8:27).*

This heaven of heavens, no human has, ascended to. The Lord alone came down from it and again ascended to it. Proverbs say: ***"Who has ascended into heaven, or descended?.. "what is His name, and what is His Son's name, if you know?" (Pr. 30:4).***

Therefore, the heavens that the Bible mentioned are:

1. The heaven of the birds.
2. The heaven of the stars, the firmament.
3. The third heaven, or Paradise, and
4. The heaven of heavens to which no human has ever ascended.

[25]

WAS THE SIN OF ADAM ADULTERY?

Question:

Some people say that the sin of Adam and Eve was adultery. As the Bible does not say this, therefore how did this idea come about? And what is the right answer for it, if it is wrong?.

Answer:

The origin and the source of this idea was "Origen" who exaggerated in his interpretation of the Bible using the allegorical method.

He tried to emphasise the meaning of symbols (Allegories) to include everything, even the sin of Adam, the trees of the garden of Eden. He said that the sin of Adam was adultery providing the evidence as follows:

He said that the tree of the knowledge of good and evil was in the middle of the garden, as the sexual organ is in the middle of the human body. He said by eating from the tree, it was said *"Now Adam knew Eve his wife, and she conceived" (Gen. 4:1).* He also said by their sexual sin, Adam and Eve became ashamed and hid themselves for they were naked, and they sewed fig leaves together to cover themselves *(Gen. 3:7)*. Origen furthered his idea about the sexual sin by saying that the whole world is controlled by sexual immorality.

However, this opinion has many objections:

1. He said that the tree of the knowledge of good and evil was in the middle of the garden, and likewise, the sexual organs are also in the middle of the body. So, if we consider that the sexual organ is the tree as Origen explained, the body would have become the garden, and we would have two gardens: Adam and eve and two trees (in each of them there is a tree). In this case, Adam would have eaten the fruit from the tree of Eve, and Eve would have eaten in turn from the tree of Adam. Consequently, God could not have placed Adam in the garden according to the Bible *(Gen. 2:14)*, but Adam himself becomes Eve's garden!! However, the Bible says that God placed him in the garden of Eden to tend it and keep it *(Gen. 2:15)*.

According to the allegorical interpretation, what is the garden of Eden then? And what does it mean to tend it and to keep it?

2. Also, what would be the meaning of the rest of the symbols in the garden of Eden?

What is the meaning of the river which went out of Eden to water the garden, and from there it parted and became four river beads *(Gen. 2:10)?* what are these four rivers? Also, what do the rest of the members of the body represent?

Do they represent other trees in the garden? Are the fruits of these trees allowed?

3. The tree of life was also in the middle of the garden *(Gen. 2:9)*.

The tree of the knowledge of good and evil was not alone in the center of the garden. Does the tree of life represent also something in the body if we went along with Origen? How can we understand then the meaning of the Cherubim guarding the way to the tree of life by flaming sword *(Gen. 3:24)*.

4. How can we understand the dismissal of man from the garden if the garden symbolised his body?

How did he depart or was driven out of it? And how could he live outside his body? How then did he separate from the tree of the knowledge of good and evil that was in the middle of the garden (his body)?

Origen's allegorical interpretation cannot provide any meaningful understanding, but it only causes endless confusions.

An important question we put before us if the sin was adultery.

5. If Adam's sin was adultery what was the commandment? Did Adam understand it?

Was the commandment *"Do not commit adultery"* and Adam disobeyed it? What could Adam and Eve understand from a statement that says *"do not commit adultery"*? as they were simple and innocent, and they did know the meaning of such a statement. The evidence for their innocence was that they were naked but were not ashamed *(Gen. 2:25)*. Did God explain for them the meaning of such a commandment?

This is impossible, for God Himself would have opened their own eyes!! God forbid.

Was there no commandment? This would be against the Scripture. Did they not understand the commandment? In this case, there would be no punishment, and the commandment would be meaningless.

6. If the sin was adultery, they would have committed this sin at the same time.

What is the meaning therefore of Eve taking of the fruit and eating it, and then giving it to Adam? *(Gen. 3:6)* If the sin was adultery, they would have eaten of the fruit at the same time.

7. The phrase *"And the eyes of them both were opened, and they knew that they were naked"* (Gen. 3:7) was after eating the fruit.

If the sin was adultery, their eyes would have been opened first to know that they were naked, and then they would commit the sin of Adultery. Since, it was impossible for them to commit a sin as this with their eyes closed.

8. Shame and the knowing of Adam to Eve was not their sin, but the sin was in their downgrading themselves to the level of the flesh in lusting food.

For this reason, it was said that Adam knew Eve his wife after they had been driven out of the garden *(Gen. 4:1)*. This did not happen in the garden. This shame also was after eating of the fruit and not during or before eating of it.

Adam was spiritually free of the lust for material things, and of eating, and of the sensual lusts. When all these things happened by eating from the tree, he downgraded himself to the level of the lust of flesh, and it became easier for him to complete the works of the flesh by committing the sexual act. This happened due to the fall, but it is not the fall itself.

9. If we could consider that the sexual relationship between Adam and Eve was a sin of adultery, then what is the meaning of *(Gen. 1:28)* **"Be fruitful, and multiply, and fill the earth..."**

This blessing was mentioned on the sixth day, before the Bible said *(Gen. 1:31) "And God saw, that every thing, that He made, and behold it was very good..."*

10. If the sin was adultery, then there was no need for the enticement of the devil to Eve to become like God.

The enticement of the serpent to Eve was not to commit adultery, but it was to become like God knowing good and evil *(Gen. 3:5)*. The sin was sin of pride. It was the desire to become equal to God. In the same sin, Satan himself fell, when he said in his heart *"I will be like the Most High (Is. 14:14)*.

In this sin, the sin of becoming like God, Eve fell then Adam followed her.

11. The wide spread of the sin of adultery today is like the wide spread of many other sins...

The love of greatness, the love to possess, the love of one's self, the love of wealth, the love to eat (gluttony), anger, lying... all these sins are widespread even in the young age (who have no knowledge of the sin of adultery) and in very advanced age (incapable to commit that sin).

12. To say that the sin of Adam and Eve was adultery is groundless.

It developed through the unacceptable allegorical way of interpretation. The allegorical way of interpretation has its own beauty and depth, only if it is supported by the Scriptures.

(*See my book "Adam and Eve" which analyses Adam and Eve's sins into 27 sins)

[26]

WHO IS MELCHIZEDEK?

Question:

Who is Melchizedek? What is the meaning of what is said in the psalm *"You are a priest forever According to the order of Melchizedek." (Ps. 110:4).* **What is the order of Melchizedek?**

Answer:

The first time that the name Melchizedek was mentioned in the Bible was when he received our father Abraham on his way back from the defeat of Chedorlaomer and the kings that were with him *(Gen. 14:17-20).* On this occasion it was said about Melchizedek that:

1. He was king of Salem (probably Jerusalem).

2. He was the priest of the most high God and that he brought out bread and wine.

3. He blessed Abraham and Abraham gave him his tithes.

St. Paul acknowledged Melchizedek is greater than Abraham.

For the inferior is blessed by the superior *(Heb. 7:7),* and that Abraham gave him tithes. Accordingly, the priesthood of Melchizedek is greater than that of Aaron (who is the posterity of Abraham).

The priesthood of Christ and of Christianity is according to the order of Melchizedek for the following points:

1. It is priesthood that offers bread and wine and not animal sacrifices. For the animal (or the bloody) sacrifices, were according to the order of Aaron's priesthood. It symbolised the sacrifice of Christ, and was abolished by the sacrifice of Christ on the cross. Christ instituted for us the sacrament of Eucharist (Body and Blood) by bread and wine according to the order of Melchizedek.

2. It is a priesthood that is not inherited. Christ was from the tribe of Judah (according to the flesh), and He was not from the tribe of Levi from whom was the Aaronic priesthood. Christ did not inherit the priesthood, neither did all the apostles of Christ. All the priests in the New Testament do not inherit their priesthood.

3. The priesthood of Melchizedek is higher than the Aaronic priesthood. St. Paul explained this point in *(Heb. 7)*.

It was said about Melchizedek that he was in the likeness of the Son of God.

This is true from the points that have been mentioned. St. Paul says also about him " *without father, without mother, without genealogy, having neither beginning of days nor end of life, but made like the Son of God, remains a priest continually." (Heb. 7:3).*

We should not take these words literally, otherwise Melchizedek would be God.

Even literally we cannot say that he is like the Son of God, because he has no father, but Christ has a father, the Heavenly Father, and he had no mother while Christ Has a mother, the Virgin St. Mary.

But Melchizedek had no father, no mother, no descent in his priesthood.

In other words he did not get his priesthood through his descent from a father or a mother and so is Christ. This coincides with what St. Paul said *" And indeed those who are of the sons of Levi, who receive the priesthood, have a commandment to receive tithes from the people according to the law, that is, from their brethren, though they have come from the loins of Abraham; but he whose genealogy is not derived from them received tithes from Abraham and blessed him who had the promises." (Heb. 7:5 & 6).*

This means that Melchizedek did not descend from Aaron, or from the tribe of priesthood and the expression *"with no father and no mother"* means the same.

St. Paul explained further by applying this statement to Christ *"For He of whom these things are spoken belongs to another tribe, from which no man has officiated at the altar." (Heb. 7:13).*

Furthermore, the Scriptures did not mention anything about the descent of Melchizedek, who was his father or mother. As if the Scripture says about him "Without father that we know of, or mother that we are acquainted with".

The Bible said also about him *"Having neither beginning of days nor end of life... "*

This means that he entered the history abruptly, and left it also abruptly without knowing the beginning of his days nor the end of his life. He appeared at a certain time to accomplish a mission and to become a symbol, without knowing his history or descent.

But Christ on the other hand, according to the flesh, His days are known.

The day of His birth, the day of His death on the cross and the day of His ascension are known. However, according to His Divinity, He has no beginning nor end.

Nevertheless, Melchizedek did not typify Christ according to His Divinity. His mention in the Scriptures *(Gen. 14; Ps. 110 & Heb. 7)* was only for his priestly function.

The opinion that says that Melchizedek was Christ Himself, has several objections: the saying of the apostle that he is like the Son of God, and that he is after the similitude of Melchizedek, and after the order of Melchizedek *(Heb. 7:3,15 & 17)*. If he is the same person, the apostle would not have said "like"-, "similitude"-, "order".

The translation of the name indicates also that Christ is not the same person Melchizedek.

His name's meaning is the king of peace or the king of righteousness, does not mean Christ, but a mere symbol.

The translation of names as to their relation to God reflects wonders:

Elija	: My God is Yahweh.
Elishah	: God is salvation.
Isiah	: God saves Elihu: He is God *(Job 32:2)*.
Samuel:	: The name of God or God hears.
Elijah	: God is father *(Num. 1:9)*.
Elizur	: God is rock *(Num. 1:5)*.
Elimelech	: God is king *(Ru. 1:2)*.
Elisha	:God is salvation *(2 Sam. 5:15)*.

No one of these people claimed, in regard of his name, to be appearances of God in the Old Testament. We should also reflect on the meaning of the angel's name and many other names in the Old Testament, but the time is lacking.

The personality of Melchizedek is one of the personalities that baffled the Bible scholars.

Many arguments have been made, most of which are contradictory. It suffices for us to say that it is a symbol of the priesthood of Christ without going into the details which would lead to misconceptions and misunderstandings, and which the Bible does not substantiate.

[27]
DO NOT BE OVERLY RIGHTEOUS

Question:

What is the meaning of the saying of the Bible *"Do not be overly righteous"*?

Answer:

The saying of the Bible *" Do not be overly righteous, Nor be overly wise " (Eccl. 7:16),* does not mean the person should not grow spiritually and does not mean there is a behaviour higher than the righteousness that God requires from us.

It means that the person behave within his spiritual level without spiritual jumps, otherwise he could be bit by a strike of self-righteousness.

The spiritual person does not *"think of himself more highly than he ought to think, but to think soberly" (Rom. 12:3)*. Don't walk in the way of righteousness over zealously but step by step until you reach. The evil can easily fight with strikes of self-righteousness pushing a person to higher degrees that he spiritually cannot sustain. The person will be unable to continue, then falls into distress and despair. During his short practice in these spiritual levels he might fall into arrogance and judging others. He will murmur against his spiritual father as if he does not wish perfection for him.

So do not be righteous in your eyes, do not be overly wise, go on slowly and quietly without jumping into levels that you might not be able to continue in, and then might be troubled spiritually.

[28]

DID JUDAS PARTAKE OF THE HOLY COMMUNION?

Question:

Did Judas partake of the Holy Communion along with the disciples on Maundy Thursday?.

Answer:

The opinion of the fathers of the church is that he attended the Passover but not the Eucharist.

This is clear from the saying of the Lord Christ about His betrayer *"It is one of the twelve, who dips with Me in the dish." (Mark 14:20)*. The phrase *"dips... in the dish"* goes along with the Passover but not partaking from the body and blood of the Lord where He broke the bread and gave them, then tasted from the cup and gave them. *(1 Cor. 11:23-25)*.

The Gospel of St. John said *"having dipped the bread He gave it to Judas Iscariot... now after the piece of bread, Satan entered him... having received the piece of bread, he then went out immediately. And it was night. " (John 13:26-30)*.

Clearly, in the Sacrament of Eucharist there is no dipping of bread but this was the Passover.

Furthermore, if Judas did partake of the Body and Blood, then he partook it unworthy not discerning the Lord's Body, and partook judgment to himself *(1 Cor. 11:27-29)*. However, the fathers said that he partook of the Passover only; then went to carry out his crime. The Lord gave His covenant only to the eleven disciples.

[29]

WERE SOLOMON AND SAMSON SAVED?

Question:

We know that when Samson sinned and broke his vow, Grace forsook him and he was taken captive *(Judg. 16)*. We know also that Solomon was enticed by his women, built high places for their gods and did not keep his covenant with the Lord who divided his kingdom *(1 Kin. 11)*.

Were Solomon and Samson saved? What is the proof?

Answer:

No doubt Samson was saved, and the Lord accepted his repentance.

The Lord listened to him near the end of his life, and through him He achieved a great victory, which the Lord had not achieved through him, all his life *(Judg. 16:30)*. But the biggest proof of Samson's salvation is that St. Paul put him in the list of the men of faith along with David, Samuel and the prophets *(Heb. 11:32)*.

I believe that Solomon was saved also and the Lord accepted his repentance.

A sign of his repentance is his writing the Book of Ecclesiastes in which the spirit of asceticism is evident. Moreover, the main proof on his salvation is the promise of God to David concerning Solomon saying *" I will set up your seed after you, who will come from your body, and I will establish his kingdom. "He shall build a house for My name, and I will establish the throne of his kingdom forever. "I will be his Father, and he shall be My son. If he commits iniquity, I will chasten him with the rod of men and with the blows of the sons of men. "But My mercy shall not depart from him, as I took it from Saul, whom I removed from before you." (2 Sam. 7:12-15).*

The phrase *"If he commits iniquity, I will chasten him... but My mercy shall not depart from him "* **no doubt is a proof that the Lord accepted Solomon's repentance and his salvation.**

[30]

THE MEANING OF "BE ANGRY AND DO NOT SIN"

Question:

Is the verse *"Be angry and do not sin "* *(Ps. 4:4)* a permission for us to get angry? Is that applied also to the verse *"But rather give place to wrath "* *(Rom. 12:19)*?

Answer:

The Bible says *"For the wrath of man does not produce the righteousness of God" (James 1:20),* and also *"Anger rests in the bosom of fools" (Eccl. 7:9),* and *"Make no friendship with an angry man, And with a furious man do not go" (Prov. 22:24).*

The verse *"Be angry, and do not sin"* was explained by the fathers in two ways:

1. The holy anger for the sake of God, as long as it in a spiritual manner with no trespasses, is holy in its purpose and its action also.

2. The anger of the person because of his personal faults and of the sins he committed, will result in him not sining in the future.

The saying of the apostle *"Do not avenge yourselves, but rather give place to wrath"* means to give a chance for the anger to depart from you and not give it a place to settle inside you... do not keep the anger inside you. It might turn to hatred and desire for revenge. Give it a chance to depart from you.

[31]

DID ONE OR BOTH THIEVES BLASPHEME?

Question:

Who blasphemed the Lord during His crucifixion, the thief on the left or the thief on the right? How could it he that one deserved Paradise?

Answer:

In the beginning both thieves blasphemed the Lord.

St. Matthew the Evangelist said *"Even the robbers who were crucified with Him reviled Him with the same thing." (Matt. 27:44)* And St. Mark also said *"And those who were crucified with Him reviled Him." (Mark 15:32)*

St. Luke is the one who mentioned the faith of the thief on the Lord's right hand saying *" Then one of the criminals who were hanged blasphemed Him, saying, "If You are the Christ, save Yourself and us." But the other, answering, rebuked him, saying, "Do you not even fear God, seeing you are under the same condemnation? "And we indeed justly, for we receive the due reward of our deeds; but this Man has done nothing wrong." Then he* *said to Jesus, "Lord, remember me when You come into Your kingdom" (Luke 23:39-42).*

Probably it was the miracles that happened during the time of crucifixion that changed the heart of the thief on the right.

When he saw the earth quake, the rocks split, and the heavens darken, his heart was touched as he was touched by Christ's forgiveness of those who crucified him and His prayers on their behalf. So he stopped reviling and blaspheming. He believed and defended the Lord Christ, admonishing the other thief. He declared his faith to the Lord asking to be remembered, and received the promise of Paradise.

[32]

DID THE BAPTIST DOUBT?

Question:

When St. John the Baptist sent two of his disciples to the Lord, he asked *"Are You the coming One, or do we look for another?" (Luke 7:19)* Was that doubt in Jesus person?

Answer:

John did not doubt the Lord for many reasons:

1. It was impossible for John to doubt Christ as he was the messenger before His face to prepare the way before Him *(Mark 1:2) "This man came for a witness, to bear witness of the Light, that all through him might believe". (John 1:7).*

He could not witness of the Lord unless he knew Him, and John did witness with strength *" This was He of whom I said, 'He who comes after me is preferred before me, for He was before me.'" (John 1:15).*

2. John clearly recognised Him and his testimony of Him during baptism was obvious.

When he saw the Lord Christ coming toward him he said: *" Behold! The Lamb of God who takes away the sin of the world! "This is He of whom I said, 'After me comes a Man who is preferred before me, for He was before me." (John 1:29 & 30).*

3. John explained how God guided him to recognise Him saying: *"I did not know Him, but He who sent me to baptise with water said to me, 'Upon whom you see the Spirit descending, and remaining on Him, this is He who baptises with the Holy Spirit. ' "And I have seen and testified that this is the Son of God." (John 1:33-34).*

4. It was because John knew Him and believed in Him that he hesitated to baptise Him.

Therefore when the Lord came to be baptised John tried to prevent him, saying, *"I need to be baptised by You, and are You coming to me?"(Matt. 3:14)* but he yield when he heard the Lord's words *"It is fitting for us to fulfil all righteousness".*

5. John's faith grew when he saw the Divine revelation at the time of the baptism.

"Then Jesus, When He had been baptised, Jesus came up immediately from the water; and behold, the heavens were opened to Him, and He saw the Spirit of God descending like a dove and alighting upon Him. And suddenly a voice came from heaven, saying, "This is My beloved Son, in whom I am well pleased." (Matt. 3:16-17).

6. John bore another witness when Jesus began to baptise and preach.

John's disciples came and told him, so he said "He who has the bride is the bridegroom; but the friend of the bridegroom, who stands and hears him, rejoices greatly because of the bridegroom's voice. Therefore this joy of mine is fulfilled. *"He must increase, but I must decrease. "He who comes from above is above all; he who is of the earth is earthly and speaks of the earth. He who comes from heaven is above all." (John 3:29-31).*

7. Furthermore, from the second day of the baptism he witnessed also and sent his disciples to Him.

The Bible says after the account of the baptism "Again, the next day, John stood with two of his disciples. And looking at Jesus as He walked, he said, *"Behold the Lamb of God!"* The two disciples heard him speak, and they followed Jesus ." *(John 1:35-37).*

8. Why then did John send two of his disciples to Christ saying *"Are You the coming One, or do we look for another?"*

St. John sent these two disciples to Jesus, while he was in jail *(Matt. 11:2).* When he heard about the miraculous works of Christ, he realised that his ministry was over and he was about to die. He wanted before his death to hand down his disciples to the Lord Christ. So he sent them with this massage to hear, see and then join the Lord... and so it was.

That is why the Lord said to these two disciples *" Go and tell John the things which you hear and see: "The blind see and the lame walk; the lepers are cleansed and the deaf hear; the dead are raised up and the poor have the gospel* preached to them. *"And blessed is he who is not offended because of Me" (Matt. 11:4-6).*

This message was more for the two disciples than for St. John.

About John, the Lord told the people on the same occasion:

"But what did you go out to see? A prophet? Yes, I say to you, and more than a prophet. "For this is he of whom it is written: 'Behold, I send My messenger before Your face, Who will prepare Your way before You.' "Assuredly, I say to you, among those born of women there has not risen one greater than John the Baptist; but he who is least in the kingdom of heaven is greater than he." (Matt. 11:9-11).

9. It is illogical that the Lord would say this testimony about a man that doubted Him.

Another point about St. John's faith in Christ is:

10. St. John was introduced to Christ while he was in his mother's womb.

The Bible recorded that St. Elizabeth while she was pregnant with John, said to St. Mary when she visited her *"For indeed, as soon as the voice of your greeting sounded in my ears, the babe leaped in my womb for joy. " (Luke 1:44)* John the babe leaped to the Babe inside the Virgin St. Mary. How could that be? The angel of the Lord answered that saying *"For he will be great in the sight of the Lord, and shall drink neither wine nor strong drink. He will also be filled with the Holy Spirit, even from his mother's womb. " (Luke 1:15)* .

[33]

A SWORD

Question:

How did Christ that loves peace and is the prince of peace say *" Do not think that I came to bring peace on earth. I did not come to bring peace but a sword. "For I have come to set a man against his father "* **(Matt. 10:34-35)?**

Answer:

He meant the sword that befell the believers (Christians) because of their faith.

In fact the start of Christianity incited the sword of the Roman empire, the Jews and the pagan philosophers against the believers. The saying of the Lord *"They will put you out of the synagogues; yes, the time is coming that whoever kills you will think that he offers God service." (John 16:2)* was fulfilled. The martyrdom era which lasted till the reign of Constantine is a proof for that.

There was also the division that happened between the members of the family because of the faith of some members while the others remained unbelievers.

For example, a son would believe in Christianity, so his father opposed him; or a daughter believed then her mother antagonised her. This way the division finds its way to the family between those who accepted the faith and those family members who opposed it, as the Bible said *"Father will be divided against son and son against father, mother against daughter and daughter against mother, mother-in-law against her daughter-in-law and daughter-in-law against her mother-in-law." (Luke 12:53)*.

Often the believer was faced with a tense pressure, even fight from his household members to forsake his faith. Therefore, the Lord continued his warning *"and 'a man's enemies will be those of his own household.' "He who loves father or mother more than Me is not worthy of Me. And he who loves son or daughter more than Me is not worthy of Me. " (Matt.10:36-37)*.

He spoke about the sword against the faith not the sword in the public relations.

Therefore, His saying *"I did not come to bring peace but a sword"* was directly followed by His saying *"But whoever denies Me before men, him I will also deny before My Father who is in heaven." (Matt. 10:33)*

The sword can be an element in establishing and applying the. spiritual Christian ethics.

A division can occur between a religious girl and her mother about the subject of decency in clothing and make up. The same division can occur between a son and his father about the subject of serving the church or devoting one's life to serving the Lord or about health and fasting, or many other sides of Christian behaviour and in all that, *"A man's foes will be those of his own household..."* Of the normal relation between people, the Lord said in the sermon on the mount:

"Blessed are the peacemakers, For they shall be called sons of God." (Matt. 5:9).

The Lord Christ was called *"Prince of Peace" (Is. 9:6).* When the angels announced His birth they said *"Peace on earth" (Luke 2:14).* He said to His disciples *"Peace I leave with you, My peace I give to you; not as the world gives do I give to you. Let not your heart be troubled, neither let it be afraid." (John 14:27).* The Bible says *" Now the fruit of righteousness is sown in peace by those who make peace." (James 3:18),* and *"The fruit of the Spirit is love, Joy, peace. (Gal. 5:22).*

[34]

WAS THE PLUCKING OF THE CORN EARS, STEALING?

Question:

When the disciples of the Lord Christ were going through the grain fields; they became hungry; so they began to pluck the corn to eat *(Mark 2:23)*. Was this considered stealing because they plucked ears of corn belonging to someone else without his permission or knowledge?

Answer:

This was not a theft because the Law allowed it. In this respect the Book of Deuteronomy says *" When you come into your neighbour's vineyard, you may eat your fill of grapes at your pleasure, but you shall not put any in your container. "When you come into your neighbour's standing grain, you may pluck the heads with your hand, but you shall not use a sickle on your neighbour's standing grain." (Deut. 23:24-25).*

For this reason the disciples' act was allowable according to the Jewish law and common customs. Anyone passing by could pluck corn to eat if he was hungry but not take it with him. That is exactly what the disciples did when they were hungry, they plucked corn and ate *(Matt. 12:1)*.

In fact, the Pharisees did not criticise the disciples for plucking corn, but instead blamed them because they did that act on a Sabbath *(Matt. 12:2)*, accusing them of breaking the Sabbath and not of stealing.

Therefore we should judge each act according to the applicable rules of the time.

[35]

FOR IN MUCH WISDOM IS MUCH GRIEF

Question:

Does the Bible discourage the growing in knowledge and learning by saying *"for in much wisdom is much grief?"* **(Eccl. 1:18).**

Answer:

The Bible meant the harmful knowledge that troubles man's mind.

There is information you gain, that might bring on you spiritual fights and lusts, which later on you regret having known it.

There are readings and knowledge that might bring doubts and affect one's faith. Other information, may affect one's good feelings toward others, or may lead one to judge them, and in all that, one might regret having known it.

Therefore, a person should have control of what to know and what to read.

Not every thing should be known to every one. Some things may open one's eyes on things not in his favour to know at a certain age or in certain psychological status, or before spiritual or mental maturity.

Of this and other similar cases the sage said "for in much wisdom is much grief".

As for the rest of the good and useful knowledge the doors of learning are wide open for all.

[36]

ARE ALL EQUAL?

Question:

In the parable of the land owner who hired labourers for his vineyard *(Matt. 20:1-40)*, **he gave one denari to each labourer, the one who started from the beginning of the day like those who started at the eleventh hour. Will we all be equal in wages in the kingdom?**

Answer:

Absolutely not, because it was said that *"every one will be rewarded according to his deeds" (Matt. 16:27).*

The same statement was also mentioned in *(Ps. 62:12 & Rom 2:5-7)* and also the Lord Christ said *"I am coming quickly,. and My reward is with Me, to give to every one according to his work" (Rev. 22:12)*

Since the deeds of people differ, so rewarding them should differ, *"whether it is good or whether it is evil" (Eccl. 12:14),* **"Which were written in the books according to their works".** *(Rev. 20:12).*

The righteous will differ in the reward and the sinners will differ in the punishment, for it was said about the righteous that *"for one star differs from another star in glory" (1Cor. 15:41),* and as for the sinners, the Lord said about the city that refused the word of God *"Assuredly I say to you it will be more tolerable certain land of Sodom and Gomorrah on the day of judgment than for that city" (Matt. 10: 15).* Then there is a state much more tolerable than other in punishment, as the Lord said to Pilate *"therefore the one who delivered Me to you has the greater sin" (John 19:11)*

The difference in reward and punishment befits the Divine justice.

So what did it mean that all received a denarius, equally in this parable?... **It meant that all were equal in entering the kingdom but not in the same rank**.

Everyone enters the kingdom, even those who repent in the last moment of their life, but inside the kingdom, every one will be according to his deeds, the one who gave 100 fold, the one who gave 60 fold and the one who gave 30 fold, every one according to his works.

[37]

IS IT OUR DAILY BREAD, OR OUR BREAD FOR THE MORROW?

Question:

The translations of the Lord's prayer differ, some say "our daily bread" and others say "our bread for the morrow" which one is more appropriate?.

Answer:

The Greek word "Epi-osios" has more than one meaning, even the early fathers of the church differed in translating this word.

+ St. Jerome's Vulgate translated it to "substantial bread" or "over super substantial bread" which means in Latin "panem nostrum super substantial" and so did Origen.

+ While St. Augustin and St. Gregory, bishop of Nyssa, translated it to "our daily bread" which in Latin "panem nostrum quotidianum".

+ St. John Chrysostom also used the same phrase "our daily bread" in his commentary on the Gospel of St. Matthew (Article 19 - Section 8).

+ The Coptic translation, which is considered one of the most known and trusted translations used the phrase "our bread for the morrow".

+ The English translation, (king James Version, and the New Revised Standard Version) says "our daily bread" and in the margin it says "our bread for the morrow".

I do not intend to put you in a linguistic rebuttal, as I do not want to bring up what the other fathers said in explaining the Lord's prayer for that will not benefit you in any way.

Furthermore, I do not want to make your prayer time a time for linguistic debates, so during prayers someone may attempt to raise his voice to dominate the voice of others, or to show that he knows what is better, or to make himself a leader or an example for the others to follow. This way the prayer itself will lose the spiritual goal which is the conversation with God to be a scientific rebuttal...! we do not need that in our spiritual life.

Basically, it is enough to understand one fact during the time of prayer which is that **the bread that we are asking for, is the spiritual bread necessary to our eternal life.**

We say that having in mind the following points:

1. The Lord's prayer is composed of 7 requests. The first three requests are pertinent to God.

a.   Hallowed be Your Name.
b.   Your kingdom come.
c.   Your will be done.

The other four requests concern us, they start with "our bread"... **and it is illogical for us to start our requests by asking for material food before we ask for the forgiveness of our sins and before asking to he rescued from temptations and all evil.**

2. This also contradicts what the Lord said: *.."therefore I say to you, do not worry about your life, what you will eat or what you will drink..."therefore, do not worry saying what shall we eat? or what shall we drink?... for after all these things the Gentiles ask... but seek first the kingdom of God and His righteousness, and all these things shall be added to you. " (Matt. 6:25,31-33). " Do not labor for the food which perishes, but for the food which endures to everlasting life, which the Son of Man will give you, because God the Father has set His seal on Him " (John 6:27).*

3. Nevertheless, if we need the bread we should ask for it but then we should ask for our daily bread, not worrying about the morrow. That what St. Gregory of Nyssa and St. John Chrysostom have said, we here ask for the bread not the pleasures of foods.

4. If we say "our bread for the morrow" what do we mean?

The bread necessary for our souls, our eternity and for our future life, the morrow... and here we should put in our hearts to ask for all the foods of the spirit as prayer, contemplation, love of God, contiguity to God and as partaking of the Holy Communion.

Notice here that the Coptic translation was spiritual in understanding this request.

5. If some say "our daily or sufficient bread," that means the material bread if it is lacking... or, alternatively, the spiritual bread that is needed for their satisfaction, lest they should fall into sin or luke warmness, nor more than they need lest they fall into vain glory or conceit.

[38]

THEY WILL NOT TASTE DEATH.

Question:

The Lord said *"Assuredly I say to you that there are some standing here who will not taste death till they see the kingdom of God present with power" (Mark 9:11).*

How could that be, and which kingdom did He mean?

Answer:

First we should understand the meaning of the word kingdom.

Apparently the person who asked the question had in mind the "Eternal Kingdom", so he was puzzled about how some of the living at that time would live until they see the kingdom!!.

Of course, here He did not mean the "Eternal Kingdom".

We should know that before the redemption, Satan was the prince of this world *(John 14:30),* and sin reigned, and by sin we die *(Rom. 5:14&17)* but by redemption God started to reign *"the Lord reigned over a piece of wood"*, bound Satan, saved the people from death and started His kingdom.

Then here it means the kingdom of God that spread by faith through the redemption of Christ *"and the Lord added to the church daily those who were being saved" (Acts 2:47),* so those joined the kingdom of God, the congregation of the believers.

The kingdom of God came with power, the power that came upon the disciples from above when they received the Holy Spirit. Few years, before St. Paul was martyred (year 67 AD); the kingdom of God had spread all over the known places of the world, and the people living then saw the kingdom of God coming with power.

[39]

SIGNS OF THE END OF THE WORLD

Question:

What are the signs by which we will recognise that the end of the world is near? Many speak about, and predict the time for the end of the world and even suggest dates for it.

Answer:

We shall mention here the signs that were recorded in the Bible:

The coming of the Anti-Christ

This subject is very clearly indicated in the words of St. Paul *" Let no one deceive you by any means; for that Day will not come unless the falling away comes first, and the man of sin is revealed, the son of perdition, who opposes and exalts himself above all that is called God or that is worshiped, so that he sits as God in the temple of God, showing himself that he is God. ... whom the Lord will consume with the breath of His mouth and destroy with the brightness of His coming. The coming of the lawless one is according to the working of Satan, with all power, signs, and lying wonders, and with all unrighteous deception among those who perish, because they did not receive the love of the truth, that they might be saved." (2 Thess. 2:3-10).*

There will be enormous falling away because of the wonders that will be manifested by the false prophet with the power of Satan and many will believe and apostatise from the true faith.

This falling was mentioned in the previous point *(2 Thess. 2:3)* and also in *(1 Tim 4:1) "Now the spirit expressly says that in latter times some will depart from the faith, giving heed to deceiving spirits and doctrines of demons. "* This failing away will be a severe and general one to the point that the Lord said about it *"And unless those days were shortened, no flesh would be saved,. but for the elect's sake those days will be shortened. " (Matt. 24:22).*

Although during history many things had happened, this general falling which is due to the miracles of that false prophet, did not happen yet. The Lord also said:

"For false christs and false prophets will arise and show great signs and wonders, so as to deceive, if possible, even the elect. " (Matt. 24:24).

All these will be reasons for the fall. The Lord also said about these difficult days *"Satan will be released from his prison, and will go out to deceive the nations. " (Rev. 20:7&8)*

Another sign is the salvation of the Jews ie. their belief in the Lord Christ.

When St. Paul talked about the belief of the Jews first then the joining of the Gentiles to the faith, ie. *"the grafting of the wild olive tree into the original olive tree, "* he said *"How much more will these, who are the natural branches, be grafted into their own olive tree?" (Rom. 11:16-24).* Then he said explicitly *"... that hardening in part has happened to Israel until the fullness of the Gentiles has come in, and so all Israel will be saved" (Rom. 11:25&26)* he means the spiritual salvation by their joining the faith.

Final signs which are the desolation of nature...

The Lord said *"Immediately after the tribulation of those days the sun will be darkened, and the moon will not give its light; the stars will fall from heaven, and the powers of the heavens will be shaken. " (Matt. 24).*

The Last sign is the appearance of Christ's sign in heaven...

After the desolation of nature, the Lord said *"then the sign of the Son of Man will appear in heaven..... and they will see the Son of Man coming on the clouds of heaven with power and great glory, and He will send His angels with a great sound of a trumpet, and they will gather together His elect... " (Matt. 24)* and that will be the end.

A comment on these signs: It is clear that the Anti-christ did not appear yet with his miracles, and accordingly the general falling did not happen. As the Jews did not believe yet, and the false prophets making signs and wonders did not appear either, but as of the wars and rumours of wars, these are the beginning of sorrows. *(Matt. 24:8).*

[40]

THE ACCOUNT OF THE DEATH OF MOSES THE PROPHET

Question:

If Moses the prophet was the writer of the first five Books of he Bible, how could they include the account of his death? *(Deut. 34:5-8).*

Answer:

This account was of course written by Joshua the son of Nun, and did not come at the beginning of the Book of Joshua but came at the end of the five Books to complete the story of Moses.

This coincides with the beginning of the Book of Joshua *"After the death of Moses the servant of the Lord, it came to pass.."*